**Comprehensi**
Teachers' Starter Book

Contents

Part one

Part two

PART ONE

Introduction

> To read with fluency, accuracy, understanding and enjoyment, pupils should be taught to use a range of strategies to make sense of what they read.
> *(Revised National Curriculum for English in England 1999)*

> All teachers know that pupils become successful readers by learning to use a range of strategies to get at the meaning of a text.
> *(The National Literacy Strategy Framework for Teaching, 2001)*

> Learning to read accurately and with discrimination becomes increasingly important as pupils move through their education ... [Pupils] should be helped to develop their own tastes in imaginative literature and non-fiction and at the same time to gain confidence in writing and speaking about them ... The importance of meaning should be stressed at all stages ...
> *(Scottish 5–14 Guidelines for English Language, 1991)*

> Pupils should be taught to read using a range of methods. They should be taught effective techniques for using the sources of information available to them, and making sense of what they read.
> *(English in the National Curriculum in Wales, 2000)*

> Pupils should develop the ability to read, understand and engage with various types of text for enjoyment and learning.
> *(Revised Northern Ireland Curriculum, 1996)*

The reading skills described above are those that every primary teacher aims to foster, and it is these skills that the Key Comprehension series targets.

Key Comprehension comprises five Pupils' Books and five accompanying Teachers' Handbooks, covering Years 2–6/Primary 2–7. The series helps to prepare pupils for the reading comprehension components of national Standard Assessment Tasks/National Tests (Scotland), and may also be used to prepare pupils for the comprehension components of 11+ entry tests in English to grammar and independent schools.

The Key Comprehension Starter Book is aimed at pupils in Year 2 (with substantial Year 1 revision)/Primary 2–3. It is targeted at England and Wales National Curriculum Levels 2–3, Scottish 5–14 Curriculum Level A and Northern Ireland Curriculum Levels 1–2.

Book 1 is aimed at pupils in Year 3/Primary 4. It is targeted at England and Wales National Curriculum Levels 2–4, Scottish 5–14 Curriculum Levels A–B and Northern Ireland Curriculum Levels 1–3.

Book 2 is aimed at pupils in Year 4/Primary 5. It is targeted at England and Wales National Curriculum Levels 3–5, Scottish 5–14 Curriculum Levels B–C and Northern Ireland Curriculum Levels 2–4.

Book 3 is aimed at pupils in Year 5/Primary 6. It is targeted at England and Wales National Curriculum Levels 3–6, Scottish 5–14 Curriculum Levels C–D and Northern Ireland Curriculum Levels 3–5.

Book 4 is aimed at pupils in Year 6/Primary 7. It is targeted at England and Wales National Curriculum Levels 4–7, Scottish 5–14 Curriculum Levels D–E and Northern Ireland Curriculum Levels 4–6.

Structure and components

The Key Comprehension Starter Book contains twenty-seven self-contained Units of work. In three of the Units, the information given is in pictorial or diagramatic form and the questions based on this type of information test children's understanding for interpreting pictures and diagrams. The remaining Units consist of short passages of text and the questions that follow these test children's understanding of the texts.

The texts are taken from a wide range of sources and are lively and stimulating. Care has been taken to reflect the pupils' own experience and to engage their interest. In accordance with Curriculum guidelines, the genres represented include modern and well-established children's fiction, fables, poems, plays, information texts, pictures, photographs and a map.

The questions are designed to encourage close and accurate reading of the texts and to foster an understanding of implicit as well as explicit meaning. The activities gradually become more demanding as the book progresses. The pupils' ability to skim and to scan, to order and to summarise, to pinpoint and to synthesise information is thus developed throughout the book.

For each Unit, the Teachers' Handbook provides answers to the questions, a breakdown of the comprehension skills tested in the activity, suggested cross-curricular links, a suggested mark scheme and ideas for extension work. These extension activities are often open-ended and offer a range of written assignments in a variety of genres, as well as comprehension questions of greater complexity and related language work.

The Teachers' Handbook also contains a commentary on the range of reading and teaching strategies that are needed to develop comprehension skills, national curricula correlation information, pupil and class record sheets and a Bibliography containing details of the sources of texts for further reading.

How to use Key Comprehension

Units are arranged in order of gradually increasing difficulty and, generally speaking, are intended to be tackled in the order arranged. However, each Unit is self-contained to allow flexibility so teachers may choose to take some Units out of order if a particular topic, genre or question form is relevant to current class work.

Teachers will find that some children who are confident, independent readers are happy to tackle the Units with the minimum of teacher intervention. Others, however, will need considerable support and guidance before this stage is reached. Most children will benefit if the teacher talks through the activity first and explains exactly what they are being asked to do. If the children's own reading is hesitant, they will be helped by the teacher reading the passage to them and thereby arousing their attention and interest.

Although a prolonged discussion at the end of the reading would be inappropriate, it is a good opportunity to deal with the children's questions, to pose a few tactical ones in anticipation of the printed ones that follow and perhaps discuss relevant aspects of the illustrations. When the children are comfortable with the passage, it can be helpful if the text is "put back together again" by being read aloud a second time.

The teacher may then wish to read through the questions with the children and discuss answers. In this informal atmosphere, the teacher is able to encourage and to prompt, and to praise warmly when thoughtful answers (firmly based on the text) are given. Children must be encouraged to pay close attention to the exact wording of the question and to consider it in its entirety before attempting an answer. Teachers can also help children search the text for the answer and gently dismiss hopefully inventive responses. As their confidence grows, children will be happy working together in pairs and in groups, reading the passage and questions themselves. Teachers will need to be on hand to support, guide and focus attention when appropriate. Collaborative activities can be very supportive when the members are well matched and each contributes thoughtfully, but teachers need to be vigilant to spot those who are taking without giving and simply copying the answers down.

Sequencing, cloze and multiple-choice activities lend themselves easily to consensus decisions and can be self-marked by the group from answers given in the Teachers' Handbook. This self-marking can be a learning activity too if the group returns to the text to establish the validity of the given answer where the group had made a wrong decision. Units where answers have to be given in the pupils' own words are sometimes less satisfactory as collaborative activities unless the children are sophisticated enough to benefit from the discussion and are happy to express themselves on paper independently. Pupils will find it more difficult to assess their own answer here by comparison with the suggested answers because wording may vary considerably.

The Teachers' Handbook allocates a full page to each Unit, and provides suggested answers and extension activities. Teachers may wish to give children a photocopy of the relevant page and allow children to check their own work alongside the suggested answers before going on to work on the extension activities provided on the same sheet.

Key Comprehension can be used to give children an opportunity to work in controlled conditions from time to time in preparation for the National Curriculum Reading Comprehension tests (England and Wales, Northern Ireland) and 5–14 National Tests (Scotland). Children unused to working on their own and in silence can be disadvantaged and unnecessarily stressed during such unfamiliar formal tests. Units from Key Comprehension can be used for individual silent practice, and pupils can become accustomed to the rules of "no conferring" and "no asking questions". They can also become familiar with working against the clock if the practice is timed.

Lastly, the Units form a useful basis for homework assignments where parental involvement can be guided and encouraged.

Reading comprehension terminology

Reading strategies

Skimming, scanning and detailed reading are essential strategies for effective information retrieval and to encourage full understanding and exploration of texts. All three strategies are developed during the course of Key Comprehension Starter Book.

Skimming and scanning are terms much in use since the advent of the national curricula. They are often used rather vaguely but are, in fact, two distinct reading strategies.

Skimming

Skimming involves reading swiftly through text in order to register the general outline (the gist) and omitting the detail. This gives the reader an overview of the material and an idea of where in the text, roughly, to find passages for closer reading later.

Scanning

Scanning involves rapid but focused reading of text, in order to locate specific information, e.g. looking for particular details such as dates, names, certain types of words, and so on.

Detailed reading

Detailed reading involves reading text slowly and accurately in order to reflect upon the structure, purpose, content and tone of the text. The reader reads attentively, "listening" carefully to what the writer is saying.

When tackling the twenty-seven Units in the Starter Book, pupils will have to employ skimming, scanning and detailed reading techniques on a regular basis. The questions direct pupils back to the text in order to find the answers. Pupils need to be told that referring back to the text is expected *(and is not cheating!)*. Reading Comprehension is not a memory test but an exercise in information retrieval and understanding.

Comprehension skills: literal, deductive, inferential and evaluative understanding

Key Comprehension Starter Book develops pupils' understanding of what they have read at several levels. As would be expected at this level, most of the questions in the Units test literal understanding. However, questions requiring deductive, inferential and evaluative responses are also regularly introduced. These questions test different types of understanding and encourage pupils to begin to read between the lines and interpret what they have read.

A wide variety of question forms is used to elicit a full range of responses requiring all these types of understanding.

Literal

Literal responses demonstrate the ability to understand the surface meaning of a text and to select information accurately from the text in answer to a question.
For example:

Question:	Where were Big Dog and Little Dog going when they saw the moon?(Unit 9)
Answer:	*They were going home.*

Deductive

Deductive responses demonstrate the ability to reach a logical conclusion by drawing on personal experience from beyond the immediate context of the passage.
For example:

Question:	Do you think the children were playing in the house or in the garden? (Unit 10)
Answer:	*I think they were playing in the garden because the brother was hit with the hose.*

Inferential

Inferential responses demonstrate the ability to reach a logical conclusion on the basis of information given.
For example:

Question:	How many children did Jack invite to the party?
Answer:	*Jack invited six children to the party.*

Evaluative

Evaluative responses demonstrate the ability to appraise, to form judgements and to weigh the evidence and its implications.
For example:

Question:	What do you think Stanley would like most about your house? (Unit 16)
Answer:	*(A personal response is expected here.)*

Range of question forms

The following chart summarises the range of question forms used in each Unit of work in Key Comprehension Starter Book.

	multiple choice	modelling	true/false	cloze	sentence completion	sequencing	answering in sentences
UNIT 1	•						
UNIT 2		•					
UNIT 3			•				
UNIT 4				•	•		
UNIT 5	•						
UNIT 6					•		
UNIT 7					•		•
UNIT 8						•	
UNIT 9					•		•
UNIT 10					•		•
UNIT 11	•						
UNIT 12						•	
UNIT 13					•		•
UNIT 14					•		•
UNIT 15					•		•
UNIT 16					•		•
UNIT 17					•		•
UNIT 18							•
UNIT 19				•			
UNIT 20					•		•
UNIT 21				•	•		
UNIT 22					•		•
UNIT 23	•						
UNIT 24						•	
UNIT 25				•	•		
UNIT 26	•						
UNIT 27					•		•

Teaching comprehension skills

The national curricula, *The National Literacy Strategy Framework for Teaching* and good teaching practice, enshrine the belief that comprehension skills can be taught.

> To read with fluency, accuracy, understanding and enjoyment, pupils should be taught to use a range of strategies to make sense of what they read.
> *(Revised National Curriculum for English in England 1999)*

> All teachers know that pupils become successful readers by learning to use a range of strategies to get at the meaning of a text.
> *(The National Literacy Strategy Framework for Teaching, 2001)*

> The importance of meaning should be stressed at all stages. The activity of reading should take place, wherever possible, in an appropriate context, and it should be concerned with the gaining of meaning from a suitable text.
> *(Scottish 5–14 Guidelines for English Language, 1991)*

> Pupils should be taught effective techniques for using the sources of information available to them, and making sense of what they read.
> *(English in the National Curriculum in Wales, 2000)*

> Pupils should develop the ability to read, understand and engage with various types of text for enjoyment and learning.
> *(Revised Northern Ireland Curriculum, 1996)*

So how can such relatively sophisticated skills be taught and developed?
What exactly can the teacher in the classroom do?

It is helpful to realise that understanding a text and answering accurately questions based on it involve a cluster of acquired skills:
1 detailed reading
2 search reading (skimming and scanning)
3 retrieval (identification and selection)
4 communication (speaking/writing)

Let us look more closely at each of these.

1 Development of detailed reading skills

Detailed reading (without skipping) gives the reader a clear grasp of the narrative. It enables the reader to know what the text is about, although more than one reading may be necessary to unlock the meaning fully.

Children can be helped to develop their detailed reading skills by answering questions, both orally and on paper, as teachers have long known. In the early stages a great deal of reading through the passages in the Units with the pupils may well be necessary. Dialogue and discussion, reading and talking about what is being read, help to focus a child's attention on the meaning of the words he or she may well have been reading fluently but without engagement.

Children can be prompted by a supportive teacher to return to the text just read to find the right answer to a question. Such questioning and this textual referral help to encourage focused, attentive and reflective reading.

It will also be useful to return to the text after the written answers have been completed to establish why some answers were incorrect or incomplete. Detailed reading of the text is the key to understanding it. Needless to say, detailed reading of the questions is also very important.

2 Development of search reading skills (skimming and scanning)

When a child has an overview of a text, search reading skills are needed to locate quickly information required to answer a question. The child will know that the information is there somewhere but will need to be able to read through quickly to find it (skimming) and scrutinise when found (scanning).

The ability to skim over the surface of a text in search of information is a skill that children will probably not develop for themselves without encouragement. Many children, even at secondary level, have only one reading speed when tackling printed text.

Children can be encouraged to skim familiar texts by having small-group or whole-class skimming races. The teacher poses challenges such as "Find the place where it says in the passage that David has blue eyes". Winners have to put a finger on the right place in the text. It is wise to allow several children to raise their other hand triumphantly but then to intervene and show the rest before embarking on another search.

Scanning races yield information as well as location. The challenge above would be rephrased as "Find the place in the passage where it tells us what colour David's eyes are". Winners would have to be able to locate the place in the text and retrieve the information. Children who simply remember the information get no credit here! The exercise is to *locate* the information with maximum speed.

3 Development of retrieval skills

The question in the Key Comprehension series have been carefully devised to test (in a variety of forms) literal, deductive, inferential and evaluative understanding.

Questions testing *literal* understanding will simply require children to retrieve the relevant information from the text. The clues will be lying on the surface of the text. Once children have become used to referring back to the text for the information they need (and not relying on memory alone and not making up fanciful answers), this type of question should present no great difficulties. Children should enjoy locating and retrieving the answer.

Retrieving implicit meaning by *deduction* or *inference* is much more difficult, and children need to be helped to read between the lines. Questions targeting implicit meaning will be phrased along these lines: "How do you know that Sarah is the eldest child in the family?"; "Why do you think Tom feels so sad?" Children will be helped by gentle support here as they look for hidden clues. It does help to think of deductive and inferential retrieval skills as detective work! Plenty of practice is offered in Key Comprehension and children will gain much by working in pairs and small groups and exchanging their ideas as they discuss the text. Such discussions can be monitored by the teacher who can steer them away from unprofitable avenues and aim them in the right direction with some judicious questions. If children later have access to the answers in the Teachers' Handbook, they can see for themselves points in the given answers that they may have overlooked.

Occasionally *evaluative* answers are invited, requiring children to express an opinion which must be supported by close reference to the textual evidence. Such questions are open-ended and all pupils will have something valid to say. More able pupils will have the opportunity to marshal a cogent argument and to develop a view.

Children will meet a wide variety of question forms in the Units and it can be helpful to alert them to the demands each form presents. In *cloze* activities, children should be reminded that they need to read right to the end of the sentence before supplying the missing word. Some children attempt to fill the gap as soon as they reach it, not realising that the sentence as a whole provides the necessary contextual clues.

In *sequencing* activities, children need to be assured that there is one best ordering of the parts within the completed whole. They can be guided to spot sequential clues such as "Begin by ...", "next" and "finally", for example. They must make a logical and not a random choice in sequencing.

In *sentence completion*, what is added must fit syntactically and must complete the sense of the sentence satisfactorily. The completed sentence must be accurate when cross-referenced with the text. The temptation must be resisted to add any random ending that happens to occur to the child.

Children should be warned that *true/false* activities may well lay traps for the unwary reader. Slight but significant variations of wording may render one choice unacceptable although very close to the truth. Children can be warned not to fall into the trap.

Again, in *multiple-choice* activities distracters may well be included that are very nearly the answer required. Great vigilance is necessary and all the possible choices should be considered carefully before a decision is made. It can be helpful to eliminate any obviously incorrect statements and then to concentrate on choosing the right answer from the statements that remain.

When children are *answering in their own words*, they should be reminded not to lift material straight from the passage but to answer the question clearly in their own way. Sometimes there is more than one point to be made. Children should make sure they have included all that is relevant to their answer.

4 Developing communication skills

Whether children discuss a reading comprehension activity or write their answers in carefully controlled conditions, they are developing communication skills. In pair work and in small group discussions, ideas should be shared courteously and productively, and the quality of the reading comprehension shown can be assessed by the monitoring teacher.

Answering reading comprehension questions by writing the answers can be a very challenging exercise for children with limited writing skills. It is for this reason that a variety of approaches is used to familiarise them with the kinds of structures useful when they come to answer questions in their own words.

Sometimes they are asked to copy out and complete a sentence (cloze and sentence completion); sometimes they have to select and write out a sentence from a pair or group in answer to a question (true/false, multiple choice); sometimes they have to write out sentences and captions in a logical order (sequencing). As the series progresses, they are expected to answer more questions in their own words, although more supportive exercises (from the writing point of view) are interspersed with these throughout the series.

Reading comprehension is traditionally tested by the writing of answers to questions. The development of writing skills will be encouraged not only by answering the questions in each of the Units but also by attempting the many varied extension activities in the Teachers' Handbook.

Teaching reading comprehension skills is an on-going classroom activity not, of course, confined to the English lesson. Such skills are vital if our children are to be enabled as enthusiastic, independent and reflective readers, as we would wish each one of them to be.

Key Comprehension and the national curricula

Key Comprehension and national curricula tests

Teachers may wish to use Key Comprehension Units formally in the classroom as preparation for National Curriculum Reading Comprehension tests (England and Wales, Northern Ireland) and 5–14 National Tests (Scotland).

Key Comprehension is a flexible resource and the Units may usefully be worked in controlled conditions as children become more confident about working individually and independently of teacher intervention. For some children, who are used only to working in pairs or groups, the experience of formally conducted tests can be a frightening one. Timed activities or conventions forbidding them to ask for help can be unfamiliar and bewildering.

Key Comprehension offers the opportunity of controlled practice in a supportive environment where the experience can be talked through beforehand and discussed afterwards. The overall task will gradually become familiar and the conventions understood. Children will be better prepared for formal tests if they have been given the opportunity from time to time of writing and working independently and quietly.

National Curriculum for England

The Key Stage 1 Programme of Study for Reading sets out the knowledge, skills and understanding that should be taught through a range of literature and non-fiction and non-literary texts. Key Comprehension is directed at nurturing the skills of reading a range of texts with fluency, accuracy and understanding, and thus the activities provide ideal support for the Curriculum.

The following chart draws on key phrases and concepts from the Reading Programme of Study for Key Stage 1, as set out in *English in the National Curriculum* (HMSO 1999).

PROGRAMME OF STUDY REFERENCE

Reading strategies

To read with fluency, accuracy, understanding and enjoyment, pupils should be taught to use a range of strategies to make sense of what they read. They should be taught to:

l focus on meaning derived from the text as a whole

m use their knowledge of book conventions, structure, sequence and presentational devices

n draw on their background knowledge and understanding of the content.

Literature

The range should include:

a stories and poems with familiar settings and those based on imaginary or fantasy worlds

b stories, plays and poems by significant children's authors

c retellings of traditional folk and fairy stories

d stories and poems from a range of cultures

e stories, plays and poems with patterned and predictable language

f stories and poems that are challenging in terms of length or vocabulary

g texts where the use of language benefits from being read aloud and reread.

Non-fiction and non-literary texts

The range should include

a print and ICT-based information texts, including those with continuous text and relevant illustrations

b dictionaries, encyclopaedias and other reference materials.

KEY COMPREHENSION STARTER BOOK

Reading strategies and understanding tested

Activities target reading texts for understanding: comprehension questions require literal, deductive, inferential and evaluative responses. Notes in the Teachers' Handbook identify the types of understanding tested by each question. Questions ask for answers written in complete sentences to encourage development of appropriate Standard English writing in a formal context.

Extension activities in the Teachers' Handbook offer suggestions for follow-up work including discussion ideas and open-ended activities.

Literature

Texts include recent, established and traditional fiction and poetry. Both realistic and familiar settings are represented as well as fantasy worlds and texts with language play. There are also texts from other cultures. Texts of increasing difficulty, both in length and vocabulary, enable children to be challenged in their developing ability to comprehend a range of literature.

Non-fiction and non-literary texts

Texts include a variety of non-fiction genres – e.g. instructions, explanation, alphabetical text, report, persuasive text, recount – and styles – e.g. letter, poster, questionnaire, map. Illustrations, photographs and other visual information are included and are integral to the development of comprehension skills.

13

Scottish 5–14 Guidelines for English Language

Key Comprehension encourages children to read for meaning and with understanding and thus supports the *Scottish 5–14 Guidelines for English Language* (1991). The following chart draws on key phrases and concepts from the Reading Programmes of Study Introduction and the Reading Attainment Target for Level A.

PROGRAMME OF STUDY REFERENCE	KEY COMPREHENSION STARTER BOOK
(Introduction) Learning to read accurately and with discrimination becomes increasingly important as pupils move through their education. The importance of meaning should be stressed at all stages.	Key Comprehension activities focus on developing reading with understanding.
As texts become more complex and various in form, the teacher needs to deploy a widening range of techniques such as sequencing, prediction, cloze procedure, evaluating the text, making deductions, marking text, comparing and contrasting different texts.	A variety of comprehension question forms and techniques is used including sequencing, cloze procedure, literal, inferential, deductive and evaluative question forms. A wide range of text types is included and these increase in difficulty gradually.
Reading activities should demand that pupils show an overall grasp of a text, an understanding of specific details and how they contribute to the whole, make inferences, supply supporting evidence.	Key Comprehension provides a structured framework for written comprehension tasks.
In teaching reading through all stages, in ways appropriate to pupils' ages and attainment, the teacher can focus on texts: *before reading,* by priming pupils for the task, for example by alerting them to unfamiliar content or ideas; by directing them into the task; *during and after reading,* by providing questions which ask for literal, inferential and evaluative responses; by asking them to demonstrate understanding by doing or speaking; by asking readers to use the text as a model for their own writing.	Extension activities in the Teachers' Handbook offer suggestions for follow-up work including discussion ideas and open-ended activities. Notes in the Teachers' Handbook identify the types of understanding tested by each question.
Strand: Reading to reflect on the writer's ideas and craft **Level A** Read, and with teacher support, talk about a short straightforward text showing that they understand one important idea.	Key Comprehension provides texts and questions for early formal comprehension activities.

Northern Ireland Curriculum for English

The curriculum states that: "Pupils should develop the ability to read, understand and engage with various types of text for enjoyment and learning." (Programme of Study: Reading)

Key Comprehension supports this aim by targeting reading for understanding using a wide range of texts and question types.

The following chart draws on key phrases and concepts from the Reading Programme of Study and Statements of Attainment for Key Stage 1 as set out in the *Northern Ireland Curriculum for English* document (1996).

NI CURRICULUM REFERENCE	KEY COMPREHENSION STARTER BOOK
a listening to and understanding a range of texts	Understanding of a range of interesting and enjoyable texts is tested through a structured comprehension programme.
b taking part in shared and paired reading experiences; **e** exploring familiar stories and other simple texts with the teacher, using drama, art and discussion to focus on distinctive features	The Pupils' Book lends itself to a range of classroom applications, from formal comprehension through to varied extension ideas in the Teachers' Handbook including discussion points and open-ended activities.
Level 2 Pupils read both silently and aloud a range of simple texts with some independence and understanding. They make simple predictions. **Level 3** Pupils read silently and show understanding. In texts, they recognise some of the main points and can select some appropriate information to support what they say. In talking about texts they begin to use inference and deduction to explore and appreciate meaning.	Key Comprehension provides a range of text types: stories, poems, plays, and a variety of information texts including instructions, map, graph, invitation, dictionary. Activities include questions requiring literal, deductive, inferential and evaluative responses. Question types are fully referenced in the Teachers' Handbook. Questions require pupils to locate specific details in texts, to interpret what they have read and to demonstrate their understanding.

English in the National Curriculum in Wales

Key Comprehension introduces children to a range of different text types and thus supports the requirement in the curriculum that children be encouraged to read both for information and for pleasure, and that they become familiar with different genres and types of text.).

WELSH CURRICULUM REFERENCE	KEY COMPREHENSION STARTER BOOK
Pupils should be given opportunities to: 3 read information … and make use of a range of sources of information 5 read and experience literature 6 understand and respond to stories and poems	Key Comprehension activities focus on developing reading with understanding. Understanding a range of interesting and enjoyable texts is tested through the comprehension activities.

Bibliography

The texts used in Key Comprehension Starter Book are taken from the following sources:

Fiction

Jenny's Baby Brother by Peter Smith, Harper Collins Publishers (Unit 6)

Big Dog and Little Dog Visit the Moon by Selina Young, William Heinemann Ltd (Unit 9)

The Incredible Shrinking Hippo by Stephanie Baudet, Hamish Hamilton (Unit 11)

Mrs Wobble the Waitress by Allan Ahlberg, Puffin/Viking (Unit 15)

Stanley by Syd Hoff, World's Work (Unit 16)

Peter and the Waterwolf by Pippa Goodhart, Corgi (Unit 27)

Poems

"The missing sock" by Roger McGough from *Pillow Talk*, Penguin (Unit 7)

"Friends again" by Paul Rogers from *Best Friends*, J.M. Dent & Sons Ltd (Unit 10)

"Enough" by Michelle Magorian from *Waiting For My Shorts To Dry*, Viking Kestrel (Unit 19)

"Quack!" said the Billy-goat by Charles Causley from *Figgie Hobbin*, MacMillan & Company Ltd (Unit 25)

The following items were written especially for Key Comprehension Starter Book:

The park (Unit 1)

The new house (Unit 2)

The badger (Unit 3)

The fox and the crow (Unit 4)

Jack's birthday party (Unit 5)

How to make a mask (Unit 8)

Making a windmill (Unit 12)

A jumble sale (Unit 13)

A party invitation (Unit 14)

The rabbit (Unit 17)

Map of Barton (Unit 18)

Dictionary of musical instruments (Unit 20)

Chicken Licken (Unit 21)

Art Week at St Andrew's Primary School (Unit 22)

A pet for Matthew (Unit 23)

Find out using bar graphs (Unit 24)

Invention: the vacuum cleaner (Unit 26)

Record keeping

The following record keeping sheets are provided for the teacher's convenience.

Class record sheet
This record sheet gives an overall picture of the marks gained in each Unit by every pupil in the class.

Pupil record sheet
This sheet can be used to record in detail each pupil's performance in reading comprehension. The questions set in each Unit are arranged to highlight the type of reading comprehension tested. Question numbers appear in the top part of each rectangle leaving space in the lower part to indicate that each question has been attempted by the pupil. The right-hand column provides space to record the total mark out of 15 gained in each Unit.

READING COMPREHENSION: Class record sheet

CLASS: YEAR: TEACHER:

UNITS (EACH MARKED OUT OF 15)

PUPILS' NAMES	1	2	3	4	5	6	7	8	9	10	11	12	13	14	15	16	17	18	19	20	21	22	23	24	25	26	27

READING COMPREHENSION: Pupil record sheet

NAME:	CLASS:	YEAR:

UNIT	LITERAL	DEDUCTIVE	INFERENTIAL	EVAL.	COMMENTS	MARK	DATE
1	1 2 3 4 5						
2	1						
3	1 3 4		2				
4	2 3 4 5		1				
5		3	1 2	4			
6	1 3		2 4 5				
7	1 2		3	4			
8			1 2 3 4				
9	1 2 3 5	4					
10	2 3	5	1 4				
11	1 2 3 4						
12			1 2 3 4				
13	1 2 3			4			
14	1 2 3 4		5				
15	1 2 3	5	4				
16	1 4	3	2	5			
17	1 2 3 4 5						
18			1 2 3 4 5				
19		1 2 3 4 5 6					
20	1	2 3					
21	1 4 5	2	3				
22	1 3		2 4	5			
23	1 2 4	3		5			
24			1 2 3 4 5				
25	1 3	4	2	5			
26	2 4	3	1	5			
27	1 4	3	2	5			

PART TWO

Answers, mark scheme and extension activities

Answers follow for each Unit of Key Comprehension Starter Book, together with a suggested mark scheme and suggestions for extension activities. Teachers may wish to photocopy relevant pages to allow pupils to mark their own work from the answers provided and to work on the Extension Activities suggested.

Answers

The activities often remind pupils to answer in full sentences in order to develop good practice from the outset. The answers suggested in the Teachers' Handbook are therefore supplied in full sentences where appropriate. In some places, open-ended questions invite a variety of possible answers and where this is the case, guidance is given on the kinds of response that are acceptable.

Mark scheme

The suggested mark scheme marks each Unit out of 15 to allow for some flexibility of response. Teachers may choose to award the suggested marks for accuracy of reading comprehension alone; or they may wish to reserve a part of each allocated mark for spelling, punctuation and sentence construction (for example, whether answers are written in full sentences). Pupils benefit from being fully involved in the assessment of their work. Therefore, any chosen criteria for marking should be shared with them. Towards this aim, the suggested number of marks for each question in each Unit is given in the Pupil Book. A photocopiable whole class record sheet is provided on page 18 and an individual pupil record sheet on page 19.

Extension activities

The extension activities offer opportunities for further work in reading comprehension, language work and writing in a wide range of genres. The specific skills covered are summarised at the end of each set of extension activities.

The park

GENRE	picture
READING STRATEGIES	skimming; scanning; locating information
QUESTION FORM	multiple choice
UNDERSTANDING TESTED	literal; picture interpretation
CURRICULUM LINK	geography; design and technology

1 Where is the baby playing?
   b) *The baby is playing on the swing.*   (3 marks)

2 Who is pushing the girl on the swing?
   b) *Mum is pushing the girl on the swing.*   (3 marks)

3 How many children are on the roundabout?
   a) *There are two children on the roundabout.*   (3 marks)

4 Where is the dog sitting?
   a) *The dog is sitting by the gate.*   (3 marks)

5 Where is the football?
   b) *The football is under the slide.*   (3 marks)

Extension activities

1 Draw a picture of the piece of playground equipment you like the best.
  Write one or two sentences to say why you like it.

2 a) Write down two things in the picture that begin with 'b'.
   b) Write down two things in the picture that begin with 's'.
   c) Write down two things in the picture that begin with 'h'.

3 Decide with a friend which piece of playground equipment you would like to
  make a model of. Different models made by the class could be used to make a
  model playground.

SPECIFIC SKILLS   expressing an opinion; drawing; initial sounds; making a model

The new house

GENRE	information: report
READING STRATEGIES	interpreting text
QUESTION FORM	following instructions; modelling
UNDERSTANDING TESTED	literal; spatial
CURRICULUM LINK	design and technology

The shape and size of the windows and doors can be individually chosen.
The colour of the door and curtains should follow the text. The position
of the door, windows and cat should also follow the text.   *(15 marks)*

Extension activities

1 Decide on an object at home that you like. Write down what the object looks
like, how big it is and what colour it is. Give your description to a friend and
ask them to draw and colour the object.

2 Pretend you are Jenny. Write a letter to your best friend telling him or her
where your new house is and what you especially like about it.

3 Draw and colour a picture of the front of your house. Write the name of your
house or what number it is and the road or street it is in.

SPECIFIC SKILLS   descriptive writing; letter writing; interpreting text; drawing

The badger

GENRE	information: report
READING STRATEGIES	skimming; scanning; detailed reading; locating information
QUESTION FORM	multiple choice
UNDERSTANDING TESTED	questions 1, 3, 4 – literal; question 2 – inferential
CURRICULUM LINK	science

1 b) *A badger lives under the ground.*   *(4 marks)*

2 a) *A badger is awake at night.*   *(5 marks)*

3 b) *A badger digs with its strong legs.*   *(3 marks)*

4 b) *A badger likes to eat works.*   *(3 marks)*

Extension activities

1 Find out more about a badger in a book about wild animals. Draw and colour a picture of a badger. Write down two more things about a badger that you have found out.

2 Which other animals or birds are awake at night?

   Find out about one of the animals and write a short description. Draw and colour a picture of the animal you chose.

3 Write down the opposite of these words:
   a) night   d_ _
   b) asleep   aw_ _ _
   c) weak   str_ _ _
   d) summer   w_ _ _ _ _
   e) light   d_ _ _

SPECIFIC SKILLS   research; retrieval; writing notes; writing a description; antonyms; vocabulary

The fox and the crow

GENRE	fable
READING STRATEGIES	skimming; scanning; detailed reading
QUESTION FORM	cloze sentence completion
UNDERSTANDING TESTED	question 1 – inferential; questions 2, 3, 4, 5 – literal
CURRICULUM LINK	English

1 *A crow had some <u>cheese</u> in his beak.*   *(3 marks)*

2 *A hungry <u>fox</u> saw him in the tree.*   *(3 marks)*

3 *"You have a very <u>beautiful</u> voice," said the fox.*   *(3 marks)*

4 *When the crow sang he opened his <u>beak</u>.*   *(3 marks)*

5 *The fox <u>caught</u> the cheese as it fell down.*   *(3 marks)*

Extension activities

1 Do you think a crow sings beautifully? Describe one sound a crow makes.
Think of another bird that makes a similar sound. Write a sentence about it.

2 Read the story again and talk about it with a friend. Write down what clever
thing the fox did and what was silly about the crow.

3 What do you think this saying means? 'Don't count your chickens before they
are hatched.' Talk about it with a friend. Write a sentence to say what it means.

4 a) Find three different words in the story that begin with 'f'.
b) Find three different words in the story that begin with 'b'.

5 Think of a word that rhymes with
a) fox   b) crow   c) sing

SPECIFIC SKILLS *making deductions; making comparisons; story writing; initial sounds; rhyming words*

Jack's birthday party

GENRE	photograph
READING STRATEGIES	skimming; scanning; locating and identifying information
QUESTION FORM	multiple choice
UNDERSTANDING TESTED	questions 1, 2 – inferential; question 3 – deductive; question 4 – evaluative
CURRICULUM LINK	maths; RE

1 How old is Jack?   *(3.5 marks)*
   b) Jack is six.

2 How many children did Jack invite to the party?   *(4.5 marks)*
   a) Jack invited six children to the party.

3 Where are they having tea?   *(3.5 marks)*
   b) They are having tea in the kitchen.

4 Who do you think is holding the cake?   *(3.5 marks)*
   b) I think Jack's mum is holding the cake.

Extension activities

1 Write about a birthday party you would like to have.

2 Make a list of the people you would ask to your party. Put your list in
   alphabetical order.

3 What is your favourite birthday party game?
   Write down what you need for the game.
   Write down the rules for playing the game.

4 Write down the months of the year. Ask each child in your class to put a tick
   against the month his or her birthday is in. Which month has the most
   birthdays? Which month has the fewest birthdays?

SPECIFIC SKILLS   descriptive writing; making a list; alphabetical order; doing a survey

Jenny's baby brother

GENRE	fiction: realistic
READING STRATEGIES	skimming; scanning; detailed reading
QUESTION FORM	sentence completion
UNDERSTANDING TESTED	questions 1, 3 – literal; questions 2, 4, 5 – inferential
CURRICULUM LINK	science

1   *Jenny had a baby <u>brother</u>.*   (3 marks)

2   *Jenny thought her baby brother was <u>boring</u>.*   (3 marks)

3   *Her brother made a mess at <u>dinner time</u>.*   (3 marks)

4   *Jenny wanted to <u>play</u> with her baby brother.*   (3 marks)

5   *Jenny's mother <u>likes</u> him just as he is.*   (3 marks)

Extension activities

1   Make a list of the things Jenny's baby brother was good at. Add the things to your list that you think he could do.

2   You may have a baby brother or sister, or have a friend that does. Write about a funny or naughty thing she or he has done. Draw a picture for your story.

3   a) Write down five different words in the story that begin with 'm'.
    b) Write down four different words in the story that begin with 'p'.
    c) Write down four different words in the story that end with 'ed'.
    d) Write down two different words in the story that end with 'ing'.

SPECIFIC SKILLS   making a list; scanning; descriptive writing; initial letters; suffixes

UNIT 7

The missing sock

GENRE	poem
READING STRATEGIES	skimming; scanning; detailed reading
QUESTION FORM	sentence completion
UNDERSTANDING TESTED	questions 1, 2 – literal; question 3 – inferential; question 4 – evaluative
CURRICULUM LINK	science; PSHE

1   *The boy found <u>a sock</u>.*   *(3 marks)*

2   *He found it <u>under his bed</u>.*   *(3 marks)*

3   *The sock was missing for <u>a week</u>.*   *(4 marks)*

4   *I think the boy had <u>smelly feet</u>.*   *(5 marks)*

Extension activities

1   Words often go together. Write the words that go together to make a phrase.

socks and	butter
bucket and	chips
knife and	shoes
bread and	spade
fish and	fork

2   a) Write down four words that rhyme with 'bed'.
    b) Write down four words that rhyme with 'been'.

3   Draw a picture of your bedroom. Describe what your room looks like.

4   Make a list of the clothes you are wearing. Put the list in alphabetical order.

SPECIFIC SKILLS   descriptive writing; rhyming recall; making a list; alphabetical order

How to make a mask

GENRE	instructions
READING STRATEGIES	detailed reading
QUESTION FORM	sequencing
UNDERSTANDING TESTED	inferential
CURRICULUM LINK	design and technology; art

The sentences should be sequenced in this order:

1 *Get a big brown paper bag.*

2 *Cut out two eyeholes so you can see.*

3 *Now draw a nose and mouth.*

4 *Put on the mask and surprise your friend.*

(15 marks)

Extension activities

1 Choose a story with your friends that you all like.
Make a mask for each of the characters in the story.
Act the story with your friends wearing the masks.

2 Write out the instructions for making a paper puppet on a stick. Draw a
diagram for each step. Give your instructions to a friend and see if they can
make the puppet.

3 These are clues for words beginning with 'm' but the letters are jumbled up.
Write down the words.
a) This will help you find the way.   p m a
b) There are twelve of these in a year.   t h o n m
c) This little creature is grey and squeaks. e s o m u
d) You use this to wash the floor.   o m p

SPECIFIC SKILLS	dramatising a story; following instructions; writing instructions; word meaning; spelling

Big Dog and Little Dog visit the moon

GENRE	fiction: fantasy
READING STRATEGIES	skimming; scanning; detailed reading; locating information
QUESTION FORM	sentence completion
UNDERSTANDING TESTED	questions 1, 2, 3, 5 – literal; question 4 – deductive
CURRICULUM LINK	design and technology

1 Where were Big Dog and Little Dog going when they saw the moon?
   Big Dog and Little Dog were <u>going home</u>.   (3 marks)

2 How did they think the moon looked?
   They thought the moon looked <u>sad</u>.   (3 marks)

3 Where did they plan to fly?
   They planned to fly <u>to the moon</u>.   (3 marks)

4 What did they want the list of things for?
   They wanted the things to make <u>a rocket</u>.   (3 marks)

5 Who bought the things for the rocket?
   <u>Little</u> Dog bought the things for the rocket.   (3 marks)

Extension activities

1 Draw a picture of the rocket showing how the things on the shopping list were used.

2 Make your own rocket out of junk material and paint it.
   Make a list of the things you used to make your rocket.

3 Put the things Little Dog bought in alphabetical order.

4 Write a letter to a friend telling them that you are going to the moon. Draw a picture of the rocket you plan to build and tell your friend how you are going to make it.

5 Find out about the first landing on the moon with a friend. Write down how far it is from the earth to the moon and how long it would take to travel there.

SPECIFIC SKILLS	modelling; model making; making a list; alphabetical order; writing a letter; research; retrieval; note making

Friends again

GENRE	poem
READING STRATEGIES	reading for detail
QUESTION FORM	sentence completion
UNDERSTANDING TESTED	questions 1, 4 – inferential; questions 2, 3 – literal; question 5 – deductive
CURRICULUM LINK	PSHE

1 How many children are in this poem?
   There are <u>two children</u>. (3 marks)

2 What was the brother hit with?
   The brother was hit with <u>the hose</u>. (3 marks)

3 What did the children call each other?
   The children called each other <u>names</u>. (3 marks)

4 Why did Mum come out?
   Mum came out because <u>the children were quarrelling/fighting</u>. (3 marks)

5 Do you think the children were playing in the house or in the garden?
   I think the children were playing <u>in the garden</u>. (3 marks)

Extension activities

1 Write about a quarrel you may have had with your brother, sister or close friend. Describe how the argument started and how it was settled.

2 Draw a picture of the two children in the den.
   Write a title for your picture.

3 Write down three words that rhyme with
   a) stick   b) den   c) sweet

4 a) Write a sentence to explain what 'sulk' means.
   b) Write a sentence to explain what 'mope' means.

SPECIFIC SKILLS   descriptive writing; drawing; word meaning; rhyming

The incredible shrinking hippo

GENRE	fiction: fantasy
READING STRATEGIES	skimming; scanning; detailed reading
QUESTION FORM	multiple choice
UNDERSTANDING TESTED	all questions – literal
CURRICULUM LINK	English

1 When did Simon find the hippopotamus?
   a) Simon found the hippopotamus on Sunday.   (3.5 marks)

2 What was the hippopotamus looking for?
   b) The hippopotamus was looking for some mud.   (3.5 marks)

3 What did the hippopotamus do when Simon said "tiny"?
   b) The hippopotamus got smaller and smaller.   (3.5 marks)

4 What did Simon want the hippopotamus to be?
   a) Simon wanted it to be his pet.   (3.5 marks)

Award 1 bonus mark for finishing.

Extension activities

1 Find out all you can about a hippopotamus.
   Write sentences to tell where a hippopotamus lives and what it eats. Draw a
   picture of a hippopotamus to illustrate your notes.

2 Make a list of words that mean the same as 'tiny'.

3 Write about where you think the hippopotamus came from and how it got into
   Simon's garden.

4 How many new words can you make from the letters in hippopotamus? Make
   a list of the words and compare your list with a friend's.

SPECIFIC SKILLS	research; information retrieval; note making; expressing an opinion; spelling; making a list; vocabulary

Making a windmill

GENRE	instructions
READING STRATEGIES	detailed reading
QUESTION FORM	sequencing
UNDERSTANDING TESTED	inferential
CURRICULUM LINK	design and technology; science

The sentences should be sequenced in this order:

1 Draw a square. Cut it out.

2 Cut along the lines for 10 cm.

3 Fold every other corner to the middle. Fasten with a pin.

4 Push the pin into a stick. *(15 marks)*

Extension activities

1 Use the instructions to make your own windmill.
Colour each side of your square before you cut it or decorate the card with silver paper shapes.

2 Work out with a friend how you could make a weather vane. Write out the instructions.

3 The word 'windmill' is made of two words, 'wind' and 'mill'. Join these words to make new words.

tea	pan
tooth	skate
sauce	brush
scare	pot
roller	crow

4 Find out about windmills. Write about what they were for and how they worked. Draw a picture to illustrate your notes.

SPECIFIC SKILLS	following instructions; writing instructions; vocabulary; research; retrieval

UNIT
13

A jumble sale

GENRE	poster: persuasive
READING STRATEGIES	skimming; scanning; detailed reading
QUESTION FORM	sentence completion
UNDERSTANDING TESTED	questions 1, 2, 3 – literal; question 4 – evaluative
CURRICULUM LINK	ICT

1 Where is the jumble sale going to be?
   The jumble sale is going to be <u>at the Village Hall</u>.   *(3.5 marks)*

2 What time does the jumble sale start?
   The jumble sale starts <u>at 2 o'clock</u>.   *(3.5 marks)*

3 What day is the jumble sale?
   The jumble sale is <u>on Saturday</u>.   *(3.5 marks)*

4 What can you buy at a jumble sale?
   You can buy <u>books and toys</u>. This is an open answer.   *(4.5 marks)*

Extension activities

1 Write a letter to send to parents asking them to give things for the jumble sale.

2 Find out what a White Elephant Stall is. Make a list of things in your house that you think could go on the stall.

3 Put the following articles of clothing in alphabetical order:
   scarf   blouse   jumper   trousers   vest   hat

4 Look up the word 'jumble' in a dictionary.
   Write down what it means.

5 Make a poster with a friend for a pet show.
   Say when and where it will be held, what time it will start and what animals it would be for.

A party invitation

GENRE	invitation
READING STRATEGIES	skimming; scanning; detailed reading
QUESTION FORM	answering in sentences
UNDERSTANDING TESTED	questions 1, 2, 3, 4 – literal; question 5 – inferential
CURRICULUM LINK	ICT

1 Who has Tom invited to his party?
Tom has invited <u>Ben to his party</u>.   *(3 marks)*

2 What time does the party start?
The party starts at <u>4 o'clock</u>.   *(3 marks)*

3 Where is the party going to be?
The party is going to be <u>in the Village Hall</u>.   *(3 marks)*

4 When is Mr Magic the magician coming?
Mr Magic the magician is coming <u>after tea</u>.   *(3 marks)*

5 What time should Ben's mum come to take him home?
Ben's mum should come at <u>7 o'clock</u>.   *(3 marks)*

Extension activities

1 Find out what day your next birthday will be on. Write an invitation for your birthday party. Say what kind of party you will have and where it will be held.

2 Draw a picture of the birthday cake you would like to have at your next birthday. Write down the message you would like written on your cake.

3 Write out a list of food that you would eat at a birthday tea.

4 What trick would you like to see Mr Magic the magician do? Write a sentence to say what it is.

SPECIFIC SKILLS	writing an invitation; drawing; vocabulary; making a list; descriptive writing

Mrs Wobble the waitress

GENRE	fiction: humorous
READING STRATEGIES	skimming; scanning; detailed reading
QUESTION FORM	sentence completion
UNDERSTANDING TESTED	questions 1, 2, 3 – literal; question 4 – inferential; question 5 – deductive
CURRICULUM LINK	English

1 What was Mrs Wobble's job?
Mrs Wobble's job was <u>being a waitress</u>. (3 marks)

2 What was the trouble with Mrs Wobble?
The trouble with Mrs Wobble was <u>that she wobbled</u>. (3 marks)

3 Where did the roast chicken land?
The roast chicken landed <u>on a customer's head</u>. (3 marks)

4 Why did Mrs Wobble get the sack?
Mrs Wobble got the sack because – <u>an open answer</u>. (3 marks)

5 Which food that Mrs Wobble carried is wobbly?
The wobbly food is <u>jelly</u>. (3 marks)

Extension activities

1 Pretend you are the manager in the story. Write down what you say to Mrs Wobble when you give her the sack.

2 Describe what a waitress has to do. Write about why you would or wouldn't like a job as a waitress.

3 Write out a menu that you might find in a restaurant or café. Don't forget to include your favourite things.

4 Read through the following list of things to eat:

fish and chips	jelly	ice-cream
pasta	roast chicken	pancakes
hamburger	fruit crumble	

Make two lists:
Foods for first course   Foods for 'afters'

SPECIFIC SKILLS	descriptive writing; making a list; categorising

Stanley

GENRE	fiction: historical
READING STRATEGIES	skimming; scanning; detailed reading
QUESTION FORM	sentence completion
UNDERSTANDING TESTED	questions 1, 4 – literal; question 2 – inferential; question 3 – deductive; question 5 – evaluative
CURRICULUM LINK	history

1 What did people live in a long time ago?
   People lived in <u>caves</u>. (3 marks)

2 Why didn't Stanley like where he lived?
   Stanley didn't like where he lived because <u>it was cold</u>. (3 marks)

3 Why did the rock make Stanley's head hurt?
   The rock made Stanley's head hurt because <u>it was hard</u>. (3 marks)

4 What did Stanley want to do?
   Stanley wanted to find <u>a better way to live</u>. (3 marks)

5 What do you think Stanley would like most about your house?
   I think Stanley would like – <u>an open answer</u>. (3 marks)

Extension activities

1 What improvements could Stanley make to his cave to make it more comfortable? Write about three changes he could make.

2 Find out more about how cavemen lived. Write about what food they had to eat and what clothes they wore.

3 Find three words in the story that begin with 'c'.
   Find three words in the story that begin with 'h'.

4 Write down three words that rhyme with 'cave'.
   Write down three words that rhyme with 'bats'.
   Write down three words that rhyme with 'cold'.

SPECIFIC SKILLS	scanning; descriptive writing; research; retrieval; initial letters; rhyming

The rabbit

GENRE	information: report
READING STRATEGIES	skimming; scanning; detailed reading
QUESTION FORM	sentence completion; answering sentences
UNDERSTANDING TESTED	all questions – literal
CURRICULUM LINK	science

1 What are rabbits' ears like?
Rabbits' ears are <u>long</u>.   *(2 marks)*

2 What bobs up and down when a rabbit hops about?
The rabbit's <u>tail bobs up and down</u>.   *(2 marks)*

3 Where do rabbits sleep?
Rabbits sleep in tunnels under the ground.   *(3 marks)*

4 What do rabbits eat?
Rabbits eat grass and young plants.   *(3 marks)*

5 What are baby rabbits called?
Baby rabbits are called kittens.   *(5 marks)*

Extension activities

1 If you have a rabbit as a pet, write about what you have to do to take care of it.

2 Rabbits have lots of enemies. Find out about the animals that hunt rabbits for food. Draw a picture of each animal you find and write its name.

3 Make a list of the animals that are kept as pets. Ask the children in your class which of the pets they have. List the pets in order of their popularity to see which animal is the favourite and which is the least popular.

4 How many new words can you make from the letters in rabbit? Make a list of the words and compare your list with a friend.

SPECIFIC SKILLS   information writing; research; retrieval; making a survey; spelling; vocabulary

Map of Barton

GENRE	map
READING STRATEGIES	skimming; scanning; locating information
QUESTION FORM	questions requiring answers in complete sentences
UNDERSTANDING TESTED	all questions – inferential
CURRICULUM LINK	geography

1 Is there a library in Barton?
   Yes, there is a library in Barton.   (3 marks)

2 What is the farm called?
   The farm is called Home Farm.   (3 marks)

3 Where is the school?
   The school is in East Street.   (3 marks)

4 How many houses are there in Green Lane?
   There are six houses in Green Lane.   (3 marks)

5 Which street is the church in?
   The church is in Church Street.   (3 marks)

Extension activities

1 If you lived at number 6, Green Lane and your friend lived at number 4, East Street, describe how you would get to your friend's house.

2 Find out who St. Andrew was. Write about where he lived and the date of St. Andrew's day.

3 Write sentences about two buildings that are near your house. Draw a picture of one of the buildings.

4 Draw a map of the streets and roads where your school is. Put in the names of the roads. Show where any big buildings are.

5 How do you think living in a village would be different from living in a town? Write sentences about three of the differences.

SPECIFIC SKILLS	giving directions; research; retrieval; making notes; map making; expressing an opinion; descriptive writing

Enough

GENRE	poem
READING STRATEGIES	skimming; scanning; detailed reading
QUESTION FORM	cloze
UNDERSTANDING TESTED	deductive
CURRICULUM LINK	science; PSHE

I've eaten all my vegetables.
Do I have to _eat_ my meat?   (2.5 marks)
I'm strong enough already.
Can't I _get_ down from my seat?   (2.5 marks)

I have eaten all my cabbage.
I have _eaten_ every pea.   (2.5 marks)
I have eaten my potatoes.
There's no room left in _me_.   (2.5 marks)

I've already grown _some_ muscles
I'm as fat as any tree   (2.5 marks)
So do I _have_ to eat my meat
When I'm tall enough for me?   (2.5 marks)

Extension activities

1 Draw a picture of your favourite dinner. Write down what you like to eat.

2 Draw pictures for all the vegetables you know about. Write the names by the pictures.

3 Write down five words in the poem that have 'ea' in them.

4 Write down two words in the poem that rhyme with 'me'.

5 Make a list of the children in your class. Measure how tall each person is. Write down who is the tallest in the class and who is the shortest.

SPECIFIC SKILLS   expressing an opinion; identifying and labelling; spelling; rhyming; making a survey; measuring; making a list

Dictionary of musical instruments

GENRE	alphabetical text: dictionary
READING STRATEGIES	skimming; scanning; locating information
QUESTION FORM	sentence completion
UNDERSTANDING TESTED	questions 1 – literal; questions 2, 3 – deductive
CURRICULUM LINK	music

1 Which one is not a wind or string instrument?
   A tambourine is not a wind or string instrument.   *(4 marks)*

2 What is used to make a sound on a violin?
   The sound is made using a bow.   *(5 marks)*

3 Where would the word recorder go?
   The word recorder would go after piano.   *(6 marks)*

Extension activities

1 Make a list of the musical instruments that are in school. Put your list in alphabetical order. Write down what group each one belongs to – i.e. string, wind or percussion.

2 Which instrument would you like to learn to play? Say how difficult or easy you think it would be to play.

3 Find the following instruments in a dictionary: xylophone, bassoon and zither. Write a short definition of each one and say which group of instruments it belongs to.

4 Find out about how musical instruments are grouped in an orchestra.

5 A violin is played using a 'bow'. What other definitions of the word 'bow' can you find in a dictionary?

SPECIFIC SKILLS	alphabetical order; expressing an opinion; research; making a list; categorising; homonyms

Chicken Licken

GENRE	traditional story
READING STRATEGIES	skimming; scanning; detailed reading
QUESTION FORM	cloze sentence completion
UNDERSTANDING TESTED	questions 1, 4, 5 – literal; question 2 – deductive; question 3 – inferential
CURRICULUM LINK	English; history

1 *One day, Chicken Licken was in the <u>woods</u>.* (2 marks)

2 *Chicken Licken thought <u>the sky</u> had fallen on her head.* (4 marks)

3 *Chicken Licken was <u>frightened</u> that the sky was falling.* (5 marks)

4 *Chicken Licken was going to tell <u>the King</u> about the sky falling.* (2 marks)

5 *Foxy Woxy took Chicken Licken, Henny Penny, Cocky Locky and Ducky Lucky to <u>his den</u>.* (2 marks)

Extension activities

1 The story of Chicken Licken is a traditional story. Write briefly why you think it is described as traditional. List the titles of three other stories that you think are traditional.

2 What sort of character do you think Foxy Woxy was? Say whether you would have trusted him to show the way to the King.

3 What do you think happened to Chicken Licken and her companions when they got to Foxy Woxy's den? Why? Write another ending to the story.

4 Make up names like those in the story for a pig, a dog and a mouse.

5 Read another version of the story with a friend. Compare the two versions. How are they alike? How are they different?

SPECIFIC SKILLS identifying story genre; making lists; expressing an opinion; rhyming; extended reading

Art week at St Andrew's Primary School

GENRE	information: recount
READING STRATEGIES	skimming; scanning; locating information
QUESTION FORM	sentence completion
UNDERSTANDING TESTED	questions 1, 3 – literal; questions 2, 4 – inferential; question 5 – evaluative
CURRICULUM LINK	art

1 What was special about the week at school?
It was an art week. (2 marks)

2 Where did the Aboriginal artist live?
He lived in Australia. (3 marks)

3 What patterns were on the cave walls?
There were patterns of hands on the walls. (3 marks)

4 How many colours were used in the paintings on the cave walls?
There were four colours used in the paintings. (3 marks)

5 Do you think the children enjoyed the artist's visit?
Open answer. Pupils should give reasons for their opinion and, ideally, support it with reference to the text. (4 marks)

Extension activities

1 Find Australia on a map of the world. Use an encyclopaedia to find out where Aborigines live in Australia and some more about their art. Make notes so that you can tell a friend or the rest of your class what you have found out.

2 Make patterns of your hands by following the instructions the children at St Andrew's Primary School used. Choose from the colours the Aborigines used. You will need to use coloured paper if you choose to use white paint. Display your patterns on a board.

3 Think of other ways of making patterns using your hands. Cover a sheet of paper with the patterns. Write the instructions for how you made these patterns.

4 Use reference books or the Internet to find out about what animals, birds and fishes you might find in Australia. Draw pictures of them and add captions to say what they are.

SPECIFIC SKILLS research; following instructions; writing instructions; writing notes; writing captions

A pet for Matthew

GENRE	play
READING STRATEGIES	skimming; scanning; detailed reading
QUESTION FORM	multiple choice
UNDERSTANDING TESTED	questions 1, 2, 4 – literal; question 3 – deductive; question 5 – evaluative
CURRICULUM LINK	citizenship

1 Who said Matthew could have a puppy?
   b) Jack said Matthew could have a puppy.   (2 marks)

2 How many puppies did Jack's dog have?
   b) Jack's dog had six puppies.   (2 marks)

3 What was Matthew saving his pocket money for?
   a) Matthew was saving up for a PlayStation.   (4 marks)

4 Who was having one of the puppies?
   a) Julie was having a puppy.   (2 marks)

5 Do you think Matthew's mum likes dogs?
   b) I do not think Matthew's mum likes dogs.   (5 marks)
   Award maximum marks if pupil supports opinion with reference to the text.

Extension activities

1 Which do you think would take more time to look after, a cat or a dog? Write down why you think so.

2 What could you have as a pet if you lived in a flat? What makes this a suitable pet?

3 Draw a picture of a pet you have or one that you would like. Say what you would need for it and how you would look after it.

4 Act out the play scene with two of your friends. Make sure you read your part with appropriate expression.

5 What do you think Matthew will decide to do? Write down what Matthew says to his mother and what she replies. Set it out like the play script.

SPECIFIC SKILLS	expressing an opinion; following instructions; reading with expression; writing dialogue as a play

Find out using bar graphs

GENRE	information: explanation
READING STRATEGIES	detailed reading
QUESTION FORM	sequencing
UNDERSTANDING TESTED	all questions – inferential
CURRICULUM LINK	maths; ICT

1 *Make a list of the pets you could have.*

2 *Ask your friends which animals they have as pets.*

3 *Write the list of pets down one side of a page of squared paper.*

4 *Colour a square for each pet your friends have.*

5 *Write down which is the most popular pet.* *(15 marks)*

Extension activities

1 Using the instructions for making a bar graph about food, make one for your group. List the foods in the order of their popularity starting with the most popular. Do the same using pets, hobbies or sports, or think of your own interesting question. In each case, say why you think the most popular item is the most popular.

2 Write about who might find the information shown in a bar graph about food useful.

3 Look through some non-fiction books and find some other kinds of graphs or charts or diagrams that show information. Find out what they are called and explain how they show information.

4 Make a list of other words you know that have the word 'graph' in them.

SPECIFIC SKILLS	gathering and presenting information; using data; following instructions; expressing an opinion; making lists; word roots

Quack!" said the Billy-goat

GENRE	poem
READING STRATEGIES	skimming; scanning; detailed reading
QUESTION FORM	cloze sentence completion
UNDERSTANDING TESTED	questions 1, 3 – literal; question 2 – inferential; question 4 – deductive; question 5 – evaluative
CURRICULUM LINK	English

1 *The dog said <u>hobble-gobble</u>.*   *(2 marks)*

2 *The <u>cock</u> made the sound the dog should make.*   *(4 marks)*

3 *An egg was laid by the <u>farmer</u>.*   *(2 marks)*

4 *In each verse the second line rhymes with the <u>fourth</u> line.*   *(3 marks)*

5 *The poem is <u>funny</u> because the animals say the wrong sounds.*   *(4 marks)*

Extension activities

1 Write down the five pairs of words that rhyme. Underline the parts of the words that make them rhyme.

2 Write about what you think caused the farmyard muddle. What do you think the farmer's wife might have thought about it?

3 How many animals are mentioned in the poem? Make a list and put the animals in alphabetical order.

4 Draw a picture of the farmyard with all the animals. Describe what you think the farmhouse would look like.

5 a) Write down three words that would rhyme with sheep.
   b) Write down three words that would rhyme with goat.

SPECIFIC SKILLS   making a list; rhyming; expressing an opinion; alphabetical order; descriptive writing

Invention: the vacuum cleaner

GENRE	information: report
READING STRATEGIES	skimming; scanning; detailed reading
QUESTION FORM	multiple choice
UNDERSTANDING TESTED	question 1 – inferential; questions 2, 4 – literal; question 3 – deductive; question 5 – evaluative
CURRICULUM LINK	design & technology; history

1 Where did Mr Booth live?
   a) Mr Booth lived in Britain. (3 marks)

2 In which year did Mr Spangler invent his vacuum cleaner?
   b) He invented it in 1907. (2 marks)

3 Who bought Mr Spangler's invention?
   a) Mr Hoover bought the invention. (3 marks)

4 How does a vacuum cleaner work?
   b) It sucks up the dust and dirt. (2 marks)

5 How do you think Mr Spangler felt about selling his invention?
   Open answer. Pupils should give reasons for their opinion and, ideally, support it with reference to the text. (5 marks)

Extension activities

1 Write about where Mr Spangler might have got the idea for his vacuum cleaner. Say why you think he sold his invention to Mr Hoover.

2 Draw a picture of a vacuum cleaner you have at your home or have seen at a friend's home. Label it. Write a description of what it looks like and how it works.

3 Who do you think would have used Mr Booth's vacuum cleaner? Why?

4 How do you think people cleaned their houses without a vacuum cleaner? Write about what equipment you would need and how you would use it.

5 Make a list of other household items that are different now than when they were first invented. Choose one to find out about. Make a 'Now and then' chart to show the similarities and differences.

SPECIFIC SKILLS	information writing; descriptive writing; expressing an opinion; research; comparing

UNIT 27 Peter and the Waterwolf

GENRE	fiction: from another culture
READING STRATEGIES	skimming; scanning; detailed reading
QUESTION FORM	sentence completion
UNDERSTANDING TESTED	questions 1, 4 – literal; question 2 – inferential; question 3 – deductive; question 5 – evaluative
CURRICULUM LINK	geography; history

1 Where did Peter live?
   Peter lived in Holland. (2 marks)

2 What was strange about the land where Peter lived?
   It was strange because the land was lower that the sea. (3 marks)

3 Why did the people want more land?
   They wanted more land to use for themselves. (3 marks)

4 What did the people build to keep the sea back?
   They built walls called dykes. (2 marks)

5 How safe do you think it would be to live near a dyke?
   *Open answer. For full marks, pupils should support their answer with reference
   to the text that shows an understanding of the principle of dykes.* (5 marks)

Extension activities

1 Holland is also called The Netherlands. Look up the word 'nether' in a
   dictionary and write down what it means. Say why Holland would be called
   The Netherlands.

2 Find a map of Holland in an atlas. Trace the map of the country and colour the
   area that is below sea level. Using a different colour, mark the area of land
   above sea level. Say what you think would happen if all the dykes were taken
   away.

3 Find out more about Holland using reference books or the Internet. Choose
   one aspect that interests you, such as what the countryside is like, or what
   Holland is famous for. Write brief notes so that you can tell your group or the
   class what you have found out.

4 Find pictures of the traditional dress for Dutch girls and boys. Draw and colour
   your own pictures. Describe the traditional footwear the Dutch people used to
   wear.

SPECIFIC SKILLS	using a dictionary; using an atlas; research; information retrieval; note making; expressing an opinion